D1378162

Alphabet Fun

A Is for Arrr!

A Pirate Alphabet

by Laura Purdie Salas

Mankato, Minnesota

A is for arrr!

“Arrr” is part word, part growl! Pirates from Bristol, a city in England, probably said, “Arrr.”

B is for booty.

Booty was mainly gold and jewels. Pirates stole these sparkly treasures from other ships.

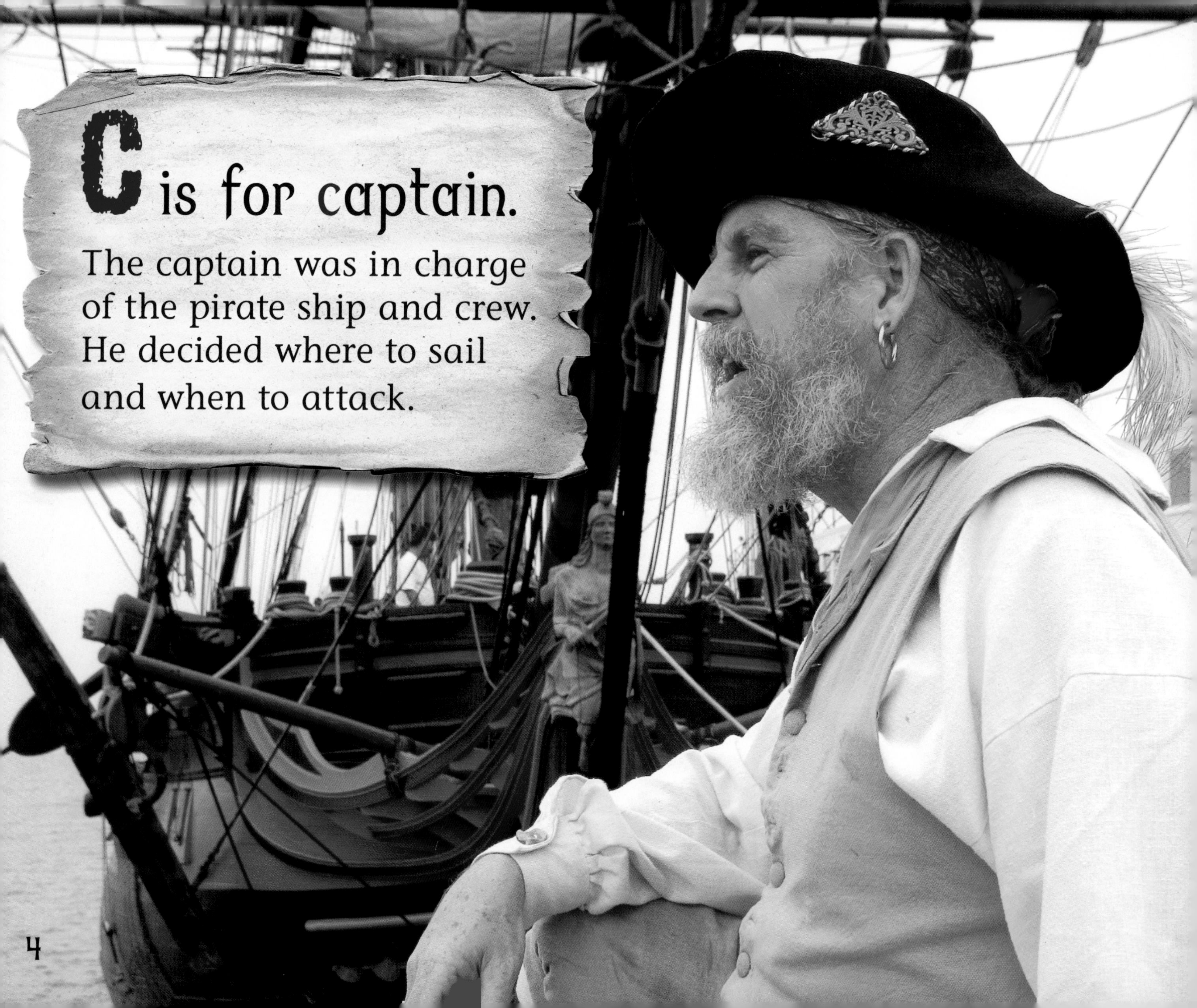

C is for captain.

The captain was in charge of the pirate ship and crew. He decided where to sail and when to attack.

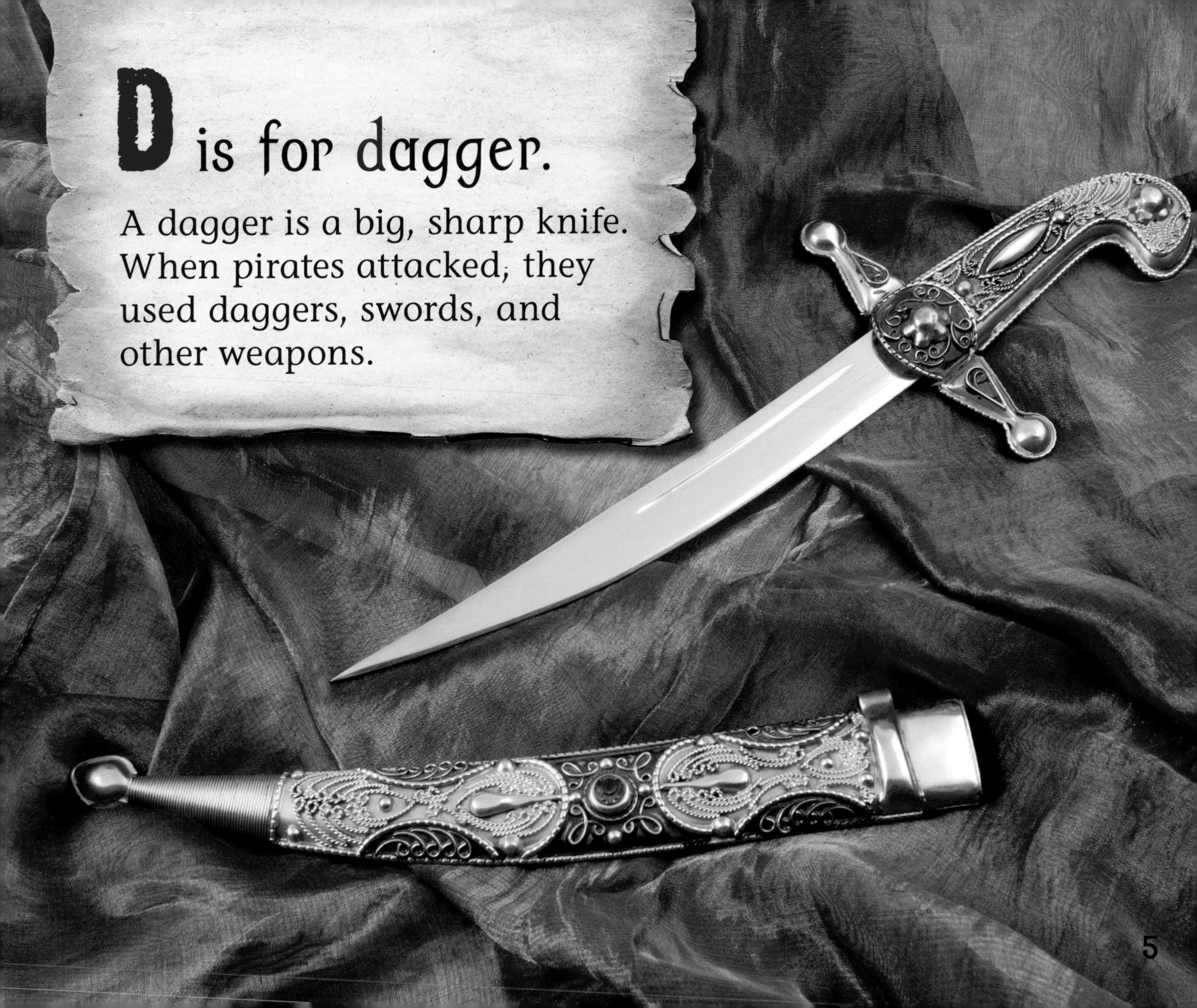

D is for dagger.

A dagger is a big, sharp knife. When pirates attacked, they used daggers, swords, and other weapons.

E is for eye patch.

Did pirates really have eye patches? Well, they did lead dangerous lives. Remember those sharp daggers?

F is for fight.

Pirates fought for treasure. They battled people on the ships they attacked. When pirates won, they sometimes kept the ships too.

G is for gold.

Spanish explorers found gold in North and South America. They melted it to make coins called doubloons. Pirates loved to steal gold doubloons.

H is for hat.

If a pirate wore a tricorn hat, he had stolen it from someone on a British ship. "Tri" stands for three, while "corn" stands for corners.

I is for island.

Pirates brought their stolen booty to nearby islands. On some islands, the deserted ones, they went ashore to stash their booty. On other islands, they spent it.

is for Jolly Roger.

rates flying this flag were
nything but jolly. When
irates raised the "skull
nd crossbones," they were
eady to attack!

K is for knot.

Pirates were sailors, and sailors tied knots. Pirates used knots to tie down sails and barrels during storms. They probably tied up prisoners too.

L is for "land ho!"

A pirate yelled, "land ho!" when he spotted land from the ship. After weeks at sea, pirates couldn't wait to go ashore for some fun.

M is for mate.

Mates were helpers. The cook and the gunner both had a mate. The boatswain, who controlled the sails and anchors, had a mate too.

N is for New World.

Pirates sailed around North and South America in the 1600s and 1700s. Europeans had just found this land. They called it the New World.

O is for overboard.

Pirates did not want to fall over the side of the ship. But during a storm or a fight, pirates could be tossed into the dangerous ocean.

P is for parrot.

Pirates sailed around the Caribbean, where parrots live. Pirates kept them as pets.

Q is for quartermaster.

Each ship had a captain. The quartermaster made sure the crew followed the captain's orders.

R is for rat.

Pirates shared their ships with rats. Rats ate the pirates' food and bit the pirates as they slept. Many ships kept cats aboard to hunt rats.

S is for sail.

Wind filled huge cloth sails and moved ships across the sea. Without sails, pirates would have been too busy rowing to steal gold.

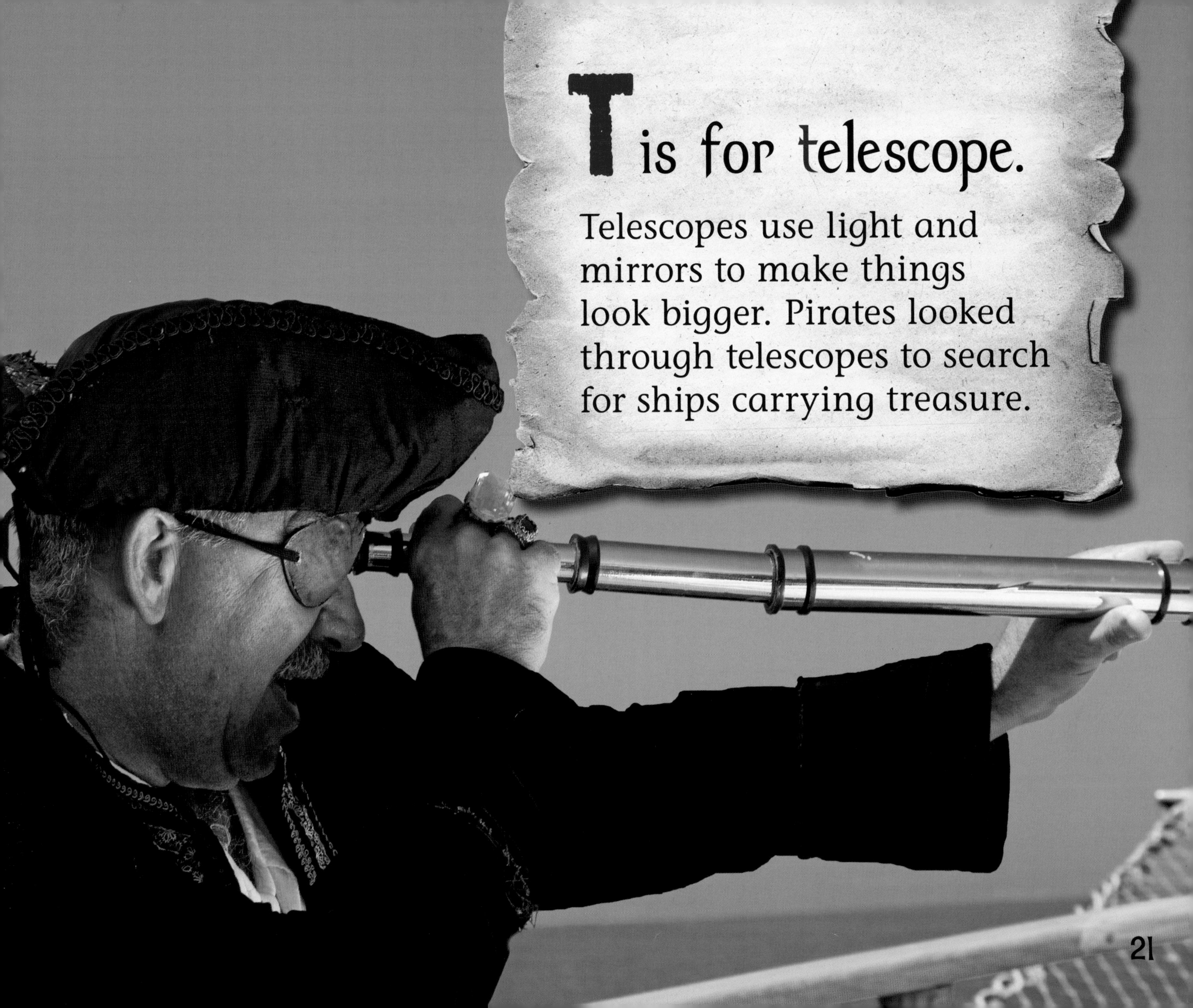

T is for telescope.

Telescopes use light and mirrors to make things look bigger. Pirates looked through telescopes to search for ships carrying treasure.

U is for underwater.

Storms and battles sank pirate ships. Sinking ships drifted down to the ocean floor. Today, treasure hunters still search for sunken pirate booty.

V is for vessel.

The pirates' vessel was a wooden ship. Pirates worked hard to keep their ship strong, safe, and fast. Their ship was their home.

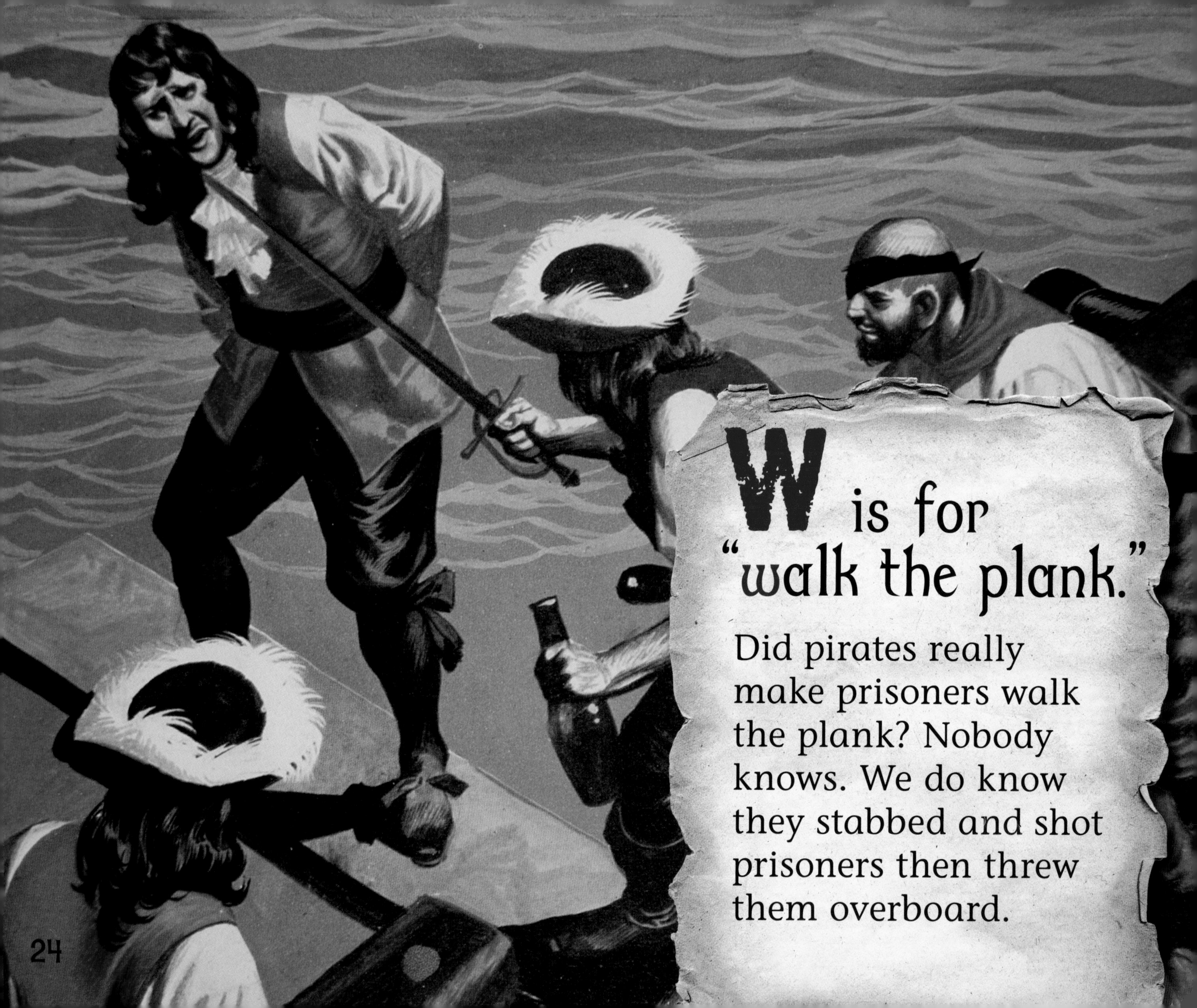

W is for "walk the plank."

Did pirates really make prisoners walk the plank? Nobody knows. We do know they stabbed and shot prisoners then threw them overboard.

X is for "x marks the spot."

Pirates couldn't stash their stolen booty in a bank. To safely store their treasure, they might have buried it. Maps helped them find it again.

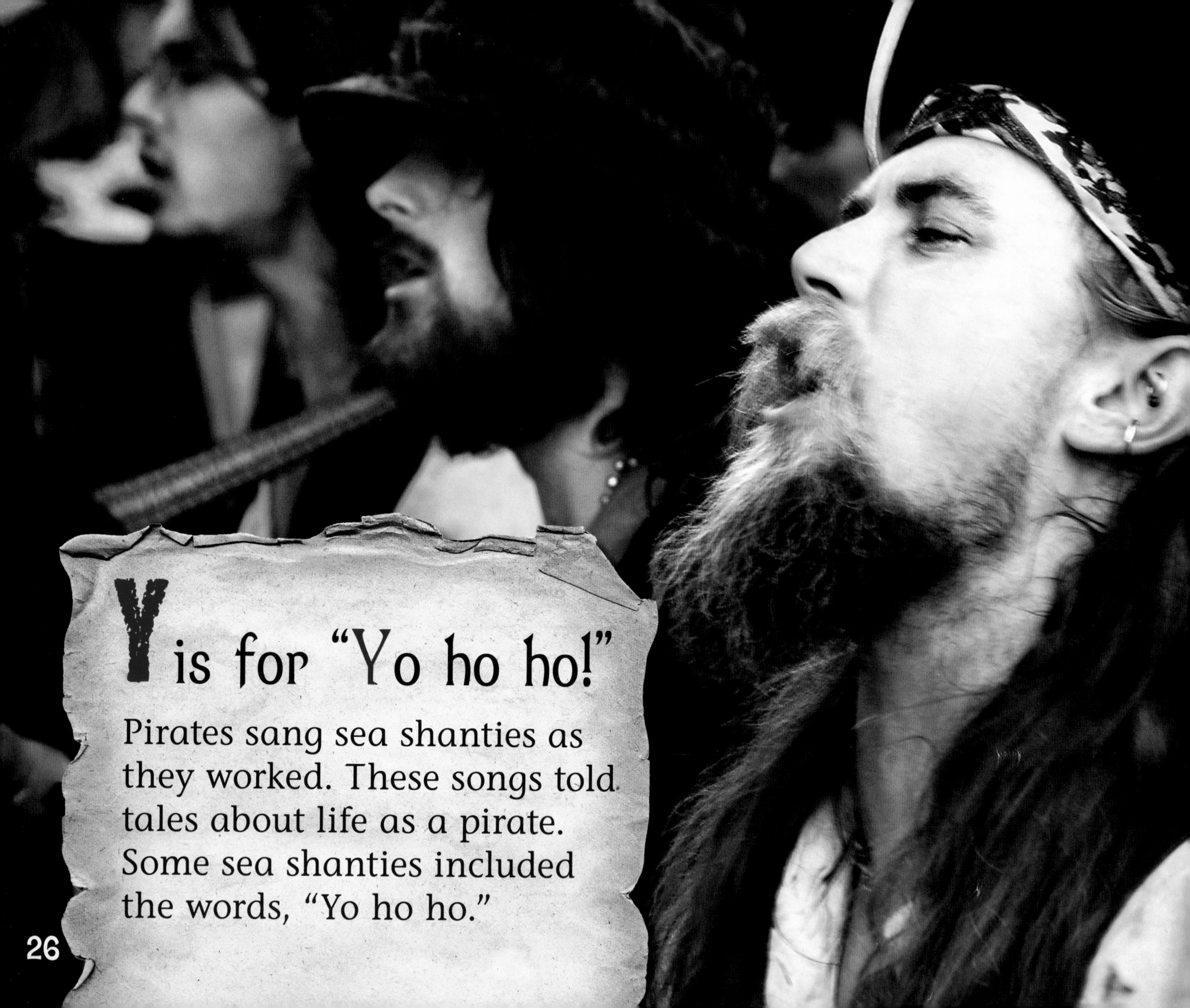

Y is for "Yo ho ho!"

Pirates sang sea shanties as they worked. These songs told tales about life as a pirate. Some sea shanties included the words, "Yo ho ho."

Z is for zzzzzz.

Even pirates had to sleep! After a long day of hiding, fighting, and stealing, they needed to rest. And the rats needed to eat. Arrr!

Fun Facts about Pirates

- Sometimes being a pirate could be boring. Pirates had lots of free time between attacking ships and stealing treasure. They played dice games to fill the hours.

- It's true that pirates stole gold and treasures. But they also had to steal everyday things, like food and medicine.

- Blackbeard was one of the world's most famous pirates. People said he placed slow-burning matches in his beard during battles. His head looked like smoke was coming out of it. The burning matches glowed red. He would have been a scary sight!

- Most pirate ships had no doctor onboard. The ship's carpenter or cook might be the only person around to try to heal hurt pirates.

- Pirates followed rules. If a pirate broke the captain's rules, the captain might leave the pirate alone on an island. The pirate would live there the rest of his (probably short) life.

- Women were pirates too! Anne Bonny and Mary Read were fierce fighters. They disguised themselves as men at first because female pirates were not allowed.

- The pirate's life was dangerous. Sword fights, guns, and cannons killed pirates. But diseases like scurvy, caused by a lack of vitamin C, killed many pirates too.

Glossary

ashore (uh-SHOHR) – on or to the shore or land

Caribbean (kuh-RIB-bee-yuhn) – the sea near the Atlantic Ocean, between North and South America; the Caribbean has many small islands.

crossbones (CRAHS-bonz) – two bones crossed over each other to make an x

disguised (dis-GYZD) – made to look like someone else through clothes or makeup

fierce (FEERSS) – daring and dangerous

gunner (GUHN-ehr) – the person on a ship who fires the weapons

scurvy (SCURV-ee) – a disease caused by not getting enough vitamin C

sea shanty (SEE SHAN-tee) – songs sailors sang

tricorn hat (TRY-corn HAT) – a black hat with three corners

Read More

Harrison, David L. *Pirates.* Honesdale, Penn.: Wordsong, 2008.

Niehaus, Alisha, and Alan Hecker. *Piratepedia.* New York: DK Publishing, 2007.

Teitelbaum, Michael. *Pirate Life.* Reading Rocks! Mankato, Minn.: The Child's World, 2008.

Internet Sites

FactHound offers a safe, fun way to find Internet sites related to this book. All of the sites on FactHound have been researched by our staff.

Here's all you do:

Visit *www.facthound.com*

FactHound will fetch the best sites for you!

Index

Note to Parents, Teachers, and Librarians

Alphabet Fun books use bold art and photographs and topics with high appeal to engage young children in learning. Compelling nonfiction content educates and entertains while propelling readers toward mastery of the alphabet. These books are designed to be read aloud to a pre-reader or read independently by an early reader. The images help children understand the text and concepts discussed. Alphabet Fun books support further learning by including the following sections: Fun Facts, Glossary, Read More, Internet Sites, and Index. Early readers may need assistance using these features.

Books published by Capstone Press are manufactured with paper containing at least 10 percent post-consumer waste.

A+ Books are published by Capstone Press,
151 Good Counsel Drive, P.O. Box 669, Mankato, Minnesota 56002.
www.capstonepress.com

Printed in the United States of America

Library of Congress Cataloging In Publication Data
Salas, Laura Purdie.
A is for arrr! : a pirate alphabet / by Laura Purdie Salas.
p. cm. — (A+: alphabet fun)
Summary: "Introduces pirates through photographs and brief text that uses one word relating to pirates for each letter of the alphabet" — Provided by publisher.
Includes bibliographical references and index.
ISBN-13 978-1-4296-3291-1 (library binding)
ISBN-13 978-1-4296-3844-9 (pbk.)
1. Pirates — Juvenile literature. 2. English language — Alphabet — Juvenile literature. I. Title. II. Series.
G535.S185 2010
910.4'5 — dc22 2009008789

Photo Credits
Jenny Marks, editor; Tracy Davies, designer; Marcie Spence, media researcher

Photo Credits
Alamy/blickwinkel, 22; David Kilpatrick, 19; Heinz Edward Schmidt, 16; MEB-Photography, 4
BigStockPhoto.com/najin, old paper background image
Capstone Press/Karon Dubke, 27
Getty Images Inc./Candela Foto Art / Kreuziger, 14
The Image Works/AAAC/Topham, 7
iStockphoto/DGID, 25; Izabela Habur, 6; Kerstin Klaassen, 21; manxman, 17
Photo of the band The Pirates Charles courtesy of Lisha Joy, torchesforghosts.com, 26
Private Collection/Peter Newark Historical Pictures/The Bridgeman Art Library International, 24
Rick Reeves, Tampa, FL, cover, 2, 9, 18
Shutterstock/Alexey Averiyanov, 12, Benjamin Howell, 15; Bryan Brazil, 10; Gene Lee, old sails background image, 20; Hydromet, background texture; James Steidl, 3, 23; Kristin Speed, 8, 28; OPIS, 11; SueC, 13; volk65, 5